Praise for Critical Therapy

When I first began writing about the terrain of radical and critical psychology, I would sometimes be asked a couple of seemingly simple questions: How can someone wary of traditional therapy's political and personal blinders actually find a critical therapist conversant with the implications of oppression and injustice, and what might a critical therapy session actually look like? Sadly, perhaps reflecting my own blinders as a privileged overeducated white man, too often I was at a loss for good answers, unable to offer much beyond vague generalizations about what kinds of questions to ask potential therapists. Over the past decade, though, the work of the Critical Therapy Institute has made answering those questions much easier, for reasons clearly outlined in Silvia Dutchevici's short new introduction to the Institute's work. Along with a useful presentation of critical therapy's core principles and an extended case description demonstrating the simultaneous focus on both personal and political transformation, Dutchevici dives headlong into two controversial topics that mainstream therapists more often push aside than address: the centrality of love and the significance of money in the therapeutic relationship. This book will lead to many conversations that need to be had.

    – **DENNIS FOX**, Emeritus Associate Professor
      of Legal Studies and Psychology,
      University of Illinois at Springfield;
      Co-founder, Radical Psychology Network;
      Co-editor, *Critical Psychology: An Introduction*

Critical Therapy is a clarion call for the therapy of our times: a just, integrative practice that refuses to treat patients outside the context of their political and social reality. This is the pathway to true individual and collective wellness. Crucial reading for therapists and patients alike.

– V (formerly EVE ENSLER), Author of
The Vagina Monologues and *The Apology*

Critical Therapy: Power and Liberation in Psychotherapy is a beautifully written book that is essential reading for clinicians working with a diverse population. By reading this book the reader will understand the tenets of critical therapy in a clear and concise manner, as well as the importance of addressing the contextual reality of the patient that ultimately would lead to an attainment of personal and structural changes for the seeker of psychological services. The author weaves her clinical experience and personal history with true caring.

– CARMEN INOA VAZQUEZ, PhD, ABPP,
Clinical Psychologist

Critical Therapy: Power and Liberation in Psychotherapy, is a well written insightful analysis of critical therapy and why it makes a stronger impact on psychotherapy patients. Like Silvia, I vehemently agree that ALL persons deserve access to therapy to support their mental health, especially those who have bigger barriers to do so because of economic hardship. As a survivor of sexual abuse and a Black woman, I know too well how difficult it is to break the intergenerational cycles of trauma. Critical therapy can be part of the long-term solution.

– NUBIA DUVALL WILSON, Author, Producer,
Mental Health Advocate

Critical Therapy is an accessible, important, must-read text for mental health professionals. It identifies the ways one can integrate a relational approach with critical consciousness in therapy and practice logistics. Inviting readers to consider what power dynamics, oppression, liberation, worth, and love mean for therapists and clients, *Critical Therapy* draws from an evidence-base of liberation psychology scholarship and a decade of practice to briefly present exemplars and recommendations. I look forward to using this as a primer in practicum classes and supervision going forward.

— CANDICE NICOLE HARGONS, PhD, Associate Professor, University of Kentucky, and Director, Center for Healing Racial Trauma

This is a beautifully written and inspiring book that includes socio-economic aspects of Critical Therapy, and makes connections between worker rights, economic equity and mental health. Dutchevici explains, for example, how Critical Therapists earn living wages, and how their sliding scale formula ensures that the waiting room is a place of diversity and equity that is often not experienced by clients in other mental health settings. So much about how we live and work produces tremendous stress because of the exploitative systems that surround us. We need to transform our society so that we engage in workplace democracy, economic cooperation and non-exploitative solidarity economics and mutual aid. *Critical Therapy* shows us how our mental health services can be part of such a transformation, and will support our liberation.

— JESSICA GORDON-NEMBHARD, PhD, Professor at John Jay College City University of NY; Author of *Collective Courage: A History of African American Cooperative Economic Thought and Practice*

As a liberation social worker, when I read the first chapter of *Critical Therapy* my heart leapt: This is the book we've been waiting for! Silvia crafts a clear map of how critical therapy honors the lived experience of those engaging in therapy, including the intersectional trauma of intergenerational violence and structural oppression. Critical therapy requires therapists to be self-reflective and accountable for their positionality, and to actively disrupt oppressive structures, while engaging authentically in therapeutic work with participants, as whole people, experts in their own lives, with agency and power. This is an invaluable handbook for therapists and participants, as they collaborate to develop healing strategies deeply rooted in values of equity, justice, and liberation. With this guidance, we can see our path to healing and transformation—of ourselves and the world.

— CATHERINE SHUGRUE DOS SANTOS, MSW,
   Anti-Violence Activist and Educator

This book lays out innovations in therapy that mirror respectful relations between human beings. Training therapists to help people grapple with how power, systems, and politics affect our mental health is going to change many lives.

— RINKU SEN, Executive Director, Narrative
   Initiative, Author of *Stir It Up: Lessons in
   Community Organizing and Advocacy* and
   *The Accidental American: Immigration and
   Citizenship in the Age of Globalization*

Critical Therapy

Critical Therapy

Power and Liberation in Psychotherapy

Silvia M. Dutchevici, MA, LCSW

FOREWORD BY
Daniel José Gaztambide, PsyD

INTRODUCTION BY
Megan Chinn, LCSW

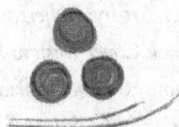

Critical Therapy
INSTITUTE

For more information, or to request permissions,
contact the publisher at: thebook@criticaltherapy.org

Paperback: ISBN: 978-0-578-37726-1
EBook: ISBN: 978-0-578-37727-8

Library of Congress Number: 2022904196

First paperback edition September 2022

Cover Art by: Roberta Zaetta
Book Cover Design: Boja
Inside Book Illustrations: George Zafiriadis (@squiddysprinkle)
Interior design and formatting: Gareth Southwell

www.criticaltherapy.org

For Adriana and Damian

Contents

Foreword

Daniel José Gaztambide, PsyD

WE LIVE in a time of crisis and uncertainty that challenges the basic assumptions of psychotherapy, from science to training to clinical practice. I remember a simple bifurcation in place during my graduate school training and beyond: Psychotherapy at its core involves a set of skills and interventions that can be applied irrespective of culture and context *and* needs to be adapted to the specific cultural and contextual needs of underrepresented and historically oppressed communities.

Whichever side you landed on this binary, it was assumed that there was such a thing as "in general" difficulties, "in general" losses, and "in general" human suffering that was distinct from culturally specific forms of struggle, historically contingent and communal losses, and a set of experiences that somehow did not fit into the category of "human suffering" —as if to say that if your suffering is "specific" to you, it is not, by definition, the suffering that "humans" experience. It might be the suffering of Black, indigenous, and other people of color, the suffering of women and LGBTQ people, the suffering of the poor, but somehow not human suffering. Is it any wonder that psychotherapy continues to struggle with the struggles we face in the year of COVID-19, sitting atop five hundred years of colonial racial capitalism?

Certain readers might feel confused by such an assertion. Certainly COVID-19 is something we are all struggling with, but isn't that separate from racism, let alone wealth inequality? I invite the reader to consider the following: We are in the midst of a global pandemic whose economic, political, medical, and societal upheaval was, if not preventable, capable of being mitigated. Why wasn't it? It is not a simple matter of stubborn politicians. A calculus was made in terms of who would be most impacted by this pandemic. Once it was determined that the most affected would be the predominantly Black and Brown and overwhelmingly poor nations and peoples of the global South, and those who are minoritized within the so-called developed world, it was all a matter of selling the idea that "it's not about me." Without question, people of color across the world and in particular the poorest and most vulnerable have been brutalized by this pandemic. On a personal level, I have no words to describe the losses and the Zoom funerals I've experienced. It is not simply that I lack the words with which to articulate them—there are no words in language capable of encapsulating a loss I could only experience digitally. We, the people of the global South, have received a five-hundred-year-old reminder that our lives are forfeit in the face of capital. But so, too, are the lives of those who have come to believe that they are safe from the pandemic.

As the number of cases and the death toll grew, more and more those who would be deemed "privileged" have begun to feel the effects of the pandemic. They find COVID-19 working its way through their communities. Suddenly, they are without healthcare or employment. Their savings begin to dwindle. They feel anxiety about tomorrow. They find themselves safe yet in an increasingly precarious situation—protected from the onslaught by working from home, yet also alienated and disconnected from others. That malaise, that uncertainty and fear, is not only the fuel that empowers those voices who seek to divide us against one another, it is also a symptom: of *capitalism* devouring the world, of *colonialism* rendering us colonized in our homes and in our minds, of *racism* circling back like a boomerang, with chickens coming home to roost. By making us unsafe, by making our lives precarious in the rising tide of inequality, you did not notice the water rising past your own ankles. Suddenly it reaches your waist, and you wonder why you are wet. Ultimately, you find yourself gasping for air just trying to stay afloat. Welcome, friend. Welcome to our world. The water is *not* fine, but it connects us. Just when you noticed the rain, we were drowning.

Traditional psychotherapy cannot even fathom the scope of the problem, let alone bridge this gap between "problems in general" and "human suffering" on the one hand, and societal injustice and oppression on the other. The former often speaks the language of relationship. The latter, often the language of power. This is precisely why critical therapy as articulated in this small volume is so much needed. Its language is brief yet concise. Its scope is both psychological and political, yet it is grounded in the suffering that binds us together. Critical therapy recognizes the deceptively simple yet profound reality that relationships are fundamentally relationships of power, and that power is negotiated in the context of relationships. In between the two lie questions of not only power but values. Who matters? Who is cared for? Who deserves, and who does not?

Critical therapy is not a call to moralism but the basic recognition that psychotherapy is textured by values within a wider network of power and relationships. It is not a therapy of moral shaming or condemnation. Critical therapy calls patients and therapists *in* to right relation, transformation, and equity. It does not "call out," for that would betray a desire to moralize and dominate the Other. Guided by a framework that synthesizes relational psychoanalysis and critical theory, critical therapy understands that most oft-misunderstood saying of Freud—"our cures are cures of love." Not love as mere sentimentality but love as action through actional dialogue. That is to say, not simply dialogue, for that might lead to what Paulo Freire warned was a form of "verbal-ism," and not simply action, for that might imply a rigid and unreflective "activism" that does not quite capture an activist ethics, but rather action in dialogue and dialogue leading to action.

In this way, critical therapy is not only a politically attuned approach but an integrative therapy in its own right. That, perhaps, is what makes it most powerful. Although grounded in a relational approach, it does not eschew integrating other therapeutic approaches (e.g., behavioral activation). Although developed out of a liberation psychology perspective, it does not seek to indoctrinate or "politicize" the patient. Rather, it draws on an array of tools and perspectives aimed not only at helping people to put words to their suffering but also to connect it to their broader relational and sociopolitical world. Isn't making meaning of our world at the heart of our work, alongside understanding how words and language fail us in the face of the ineffable? How less so is it making meaning of our *political* world, and in wrestling with how language breaks down as we try to relate with one another across lines of power and difference? Is this dialectic not the essence of therapeutic love itself?

As the author of this volume attests:

> Love for the patient and with the patient is the ultimate gift of therapy. Both patient and thera-pist change as a result of this intimate relationship, developed over time amid stories of horror, anger,

shame, fear, as well as beauty, hope and healing. Learning how to be with an Other in the therapeutic hour is the blueprint of the art of loving; the art of being with someone, of accepting the perfect imperfections of an Other, of being together.

Again, this must not be read as an "in general" statement but a resoundingly political one. Would we be caught in the throes of this global crisis if not for our structural, economic, and political inability to recognize that "thou art that"? We are all connected, even as the fantasy of a racial hierarchy makes some of us believe that we are human and others are not. Critical therapy as both intervention and lens of analysis calls on us to question binaries and bifurcations, hierarchies and power relations. This includes the bifurcation of "general" therapy and "critical" therapy itself. In this sense, the goal of critical therapy might very well be to make itself redundant. If therapy is not critical, if its cure is not a cure of love, then what the fuck are we even doing? In that respect, psychotherapy should be less a "talk therapy" and more of a "do therapy": The doing of care and justice as such.

Introduction

Megan Chinn, MSW, LCSW

I BEGAN my journey in healing work in the realm of social justice. I started a restorative justice program because I was motivated to give an alternative space to young people who were impacted by the criminal justice system and harsh and punitive discipline models in school. I found that I gravitated most toward individual work. It was soon evident that cultivating a space for people to go deeper into their lived experience and trauma allowed them to engage more fully in other aspects of their life.

I knew then that I wanted to focus on growing my clinical knowledge and practice, but the many institutes and training programs that I researched lacked any analysis of how systems, race, class, socioeconomic status, sexual identity, and gender fundamentally shape the human experience. The work I had been doing was always against the backdrop of how various systems of oppression impacted an individual's reality, so I understood and was committed to making it a foundational part of my clinical focus.

I was fortunate to be introduced to critical therapy by a mentor, and as I learned more about the therapeutic practice, I knew this was a place, theory, and practice that I could learn from and an approach I felt aligned with. This was a context where we would not only talk about personal and familial trauma but were also engaged in a deep dialogue about social and political trauma and how that should be invited into the clinical hour as an integral part of the therapeutic model. Many clinicians say that the personal is not political, but I believe that we carry our politics with us. One of the greatest lessons I have learned from critical therapy is that our politics are reflected in the questions that we ask and the ways that we ask them. This highlights the necessity to actively engage in this process, which is already present in the room.

In joining this practice, I made a commitment to continually doing the work on myself with each new patient I encountered. What critical therapy asks of the clinician is that they have an analysis of race, class, gender and socioeconomic status in the therapeutic context and engage in a power analysis in the therapeutic hour. This includes examining our own place in society as well as with our patients, and looking at how that impacts our work together. We acknowledge that this work is relational, that we arrive at truth together, and that collaboration demands a level of transparency that is hard to find in other practices.

It does not mean that there is an indoctrination of political beliefs; we simply believe in asking critical questions to examine one's experience in society. It is not that all of us who are a part of the Critical Therapy Institute have the same belief systems or same style of working, but we are grounded in a commitment to challenge the status quo and to always be on the side of the oppressed. Bringing all these factors to the surface and naming how these social implications impact a person's experience is a transformative process for both patient and practitioner. It is a humanizing process for all involved. I am grateful to be a part of this work, alongside such powerful people, engaged not only in the healing of individuals but of society at large.

Chapter One

What Is Critical Therapy, and How Is It Different from Other Psychotherapies?

I. We engage in power analysis

POWER ANALYSIS is at the core of our work. In sessions, through active dialogue, patient[1] and therapist engage in a process of critically analyzing the world by looking at power relations. Power is the "transformative capacity," the ability of people to make a difference in the world (Giddens, 1984). It exists in every relationship and is inseparable from social interactions. Power is a dynamic between human agency (the way individuals influence the world) and social structures (structures of domination that determine to what degree individuals may influence the world). It can be coercive, repressive, or negative; it can also be a productive force.

We analyze power in terms of societal structures (for example, race, class, gender, and religion) and from an interpersonal perspective (relationships, family dynamics, etc.). We look at the patient's relationship to power, and we also actively question and analyze the therapist's position of power in therapy as well as in society. Further, we analyze how power affects and informs the therapeutic relationship. In doing so, patients quickly begin to see how power manifests in their daily interactions, while simultaneously challenging therapists to check their own biases.

II. We see the therapeutic relationship as a blueprint for all other relationships

Critical therapy believes that one of the fundamental goals of therapy is to learn how to create and maintain a healthy relationship with an Other. We see the relationship between therapist and patient as one of partnership and collaboration and as a model for all other relationships. This enables patients to form more meaningful, fulfilling and authentic relationships in their own lives.

III. We believe the personal is political

Unlike traditional therapy, we invite the political into the therapeutic discussion because we believe that the personal is political and that the consulting room should be a space to analyze how politics influences and affects mental health. By the political, we mean the way power is achieved and maintained in a society—for example, how issues around workers' rights, equal pay, LGBTQ rights, parental leave, universal basic income, etc., impact and interact with one's everyday life and mental health.

In critical therapy, patients not only understand and work on their psychological issues, they also begin to see their own transformative power and understand how psychological issues interact with political ones.

IV. We practice a politics of equity

We believe everyone should be able to access high-quality, at times life-saving, psychotherapy services, regardless of income and financial resources. For the uninsured or underinsured, it can be challenging if not impossible to find an experienced psychotherapist who is a good fit. We believe therapeutic services should not be distributed according to a competitive marketplace to only the highest bidders.

Putting equity into practice, our sliding-scale model asks everyone entering psychotherapy to pay their fair share according to their income and resources. There is no minimum or maximum per session. For example, a session could cost $50 or $500. This way, the more affluent subsidize the less affluent patients.

This model also enables patients and therapists to deal with income inequality in a very tangible and personal way, enacting a politics of equity. Simply put: Everyone paying the same percentage of their financial resources for their session levels the playing field for patients and ensures adequate compensation for the psychotherapist.

Therapeutically, the sliding-scale model provokes meaningful conversations between therapist and patient about the otherwise taboo topic of money, which may foster a critical inquiry into one's personal relationship to wealth. Our society implicitly and explicitly sends the message that money is equivalent to worth, and the sliding scale challenges that by valuing people equally rather than unequally according to their earning power.

These four guiding principles of critical therapy combine modern psychoanalytic techniques with the theory and practice of liberation psychology and critical pedagogy. We seek empowerment, liberation, and healing.

The goal of critical therapy is not just analysis or the adaptation and accommodation of the individual to oppressive systems and relationships. The goal is liberation, and in the process, we help to create more collaborative relationships, workspaces, and environments and ultimately a more democratic society.

Chapter Two

Ana: A Case History

CRITICAL THERAPY is a moral project as well as a process, since it has at its core a preferential option for the oppressed and the marginalized. The commitment is always to liberation. In sessions, through active dialogue, the patient and therapist engage in a process of critically analyzing the world by looking at mechanisms of oppression and dehumanization. They begin a critique of neoliberal capitalist, heteropatriarchal, and racist ideologies by looking at the patient's position within society and their status in relation to power. They also look at the therapist's relation to power and position within society and how that affects the therapeutic relationship. Power is an intrinsic part of the dialogue, from both an interpersonal perspective and in terms of its organization in society (Burton & Kagan, 2005). The goal is to engage in liberatory praxis: to open new possibilities for action and new self-understanding; to reflect intra-psychically, socio-economically, and politically; to act and to reflect again.

Ana's Journey

Ana[2] is in her late twenties and a survivor of domestic violence. She came to the United States from Guinea-Bissau in 2010 to pursue her education. While in school, Ana met her boyfriend and has been dating him for over four years. I met Ana shortly afterward when she called me to speak about her abusive relationship. Ana reported that her boyfriend attacked her, scratched her, and broke a bottle on her head. Initially, she refused medical treatment or counseling but finally agreed after several days of phone conversations. Prior to our meeting, I advised Ana that our consultation would give both of us the opportunity to assess whether or not we want to work together. In order to facilitate the deep trust and intimacy required for psychotherapy, I believe it is imperative that both patient and therapist are intentional in their decision to work together, that they choose each other.

Ana's story is, unfortunately, typical of domestic violence narratives. Her partner was charming at first but became verbally abusive as time progressed. The abuse escalated to physical violence, and he tried to choke her.

Ana continued her therapy with me for over four years. During this time, as you will see, more stories of abuse surfaced. We talked about them, we analyzed them, and together we practiced what I now call critical therapy.

In critical therapy, as in critical pedagogy (Freire, 2000), every session is different, as every situation is different. At first, patient and therapist begin in much the same way as in traditional interpersonal analysis.

They discuss issues related to family history, intrapsychic conflict, sexual desire, and transference. In line with traditional psychoanalysis, the therapist at this stage maintains a certain distance from the patient, who invests power in the therapist, seeing them as a person who will offer guidance and relief. This investment of power facilitates fantasy and transference relations, much needed for the intrapsychic part of the analysis. At the early stages of therapy, the therapist uses this banking model[3] of therapy to learn about the inner world of the patient.

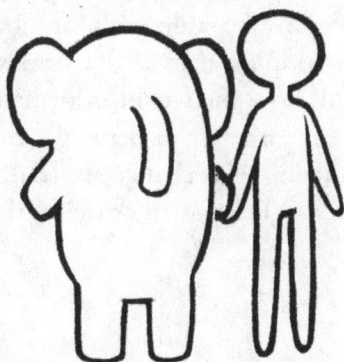

The therapist uses dreams, fantasies, projections, free association, and early memories, as well as emergent life themes, to facilitate patient insight.

Transference is an important part of this therapeutic phase. The patient's feelings for the therapist, who slowly becomes a significant figure in the patient's life, are used to show how the patient interprets and responds to current relationships and situations in ways that are similar to how they have related to significant persons in their past. By understanding how this past behavior influences and determines present behavior, the patient can learn to make more appropriate decisions. At this stage, the patient and therapist work through the transference and resistance.

Establishing trust is also an important part of the therapeutic process, especially when working with highly traumatized individuals (such as survivors of violence, trauma, and persecution) who have been deeply wounded and lost faith in human relationships. To achieve trust, the therapeutic relationship needs to encompass a level of accompaniment and transparency (Fabri et al., 2009). Accompaniment is an umbrella term that includes a family of related practices: "equality, listening, seeking consensus, and exemplary action" (Lynd, 2012). It literally means "to walk with, or alongside people" (Gates, 1988). In simple terms, it's a praxis (how theory informs the world, how the world informs theory) of being with the patient rather than being for the patient. The practice of accompaniment challenges traditional clinical boundaries (Fabri, 2001) because it criticizes the stance of the neutral therapist.

Stage One

My sessions with Ana began by establishing trust and talking about the abuse. We talked about Ana's feelings regarding her partner. She was deeply conflicted about her love and hate for him. When she started therapy, Ana was dependent on her boyfriend, and this dependency further complicated Ana's feelings and relationship with him. Although they did not live together, he provided some financial assistance for food, clothing, etc. Ana could not work more than twenty hours a week because she was on a student visa. The money she earned from her work, with a minimum wage salary, went toward her tuition, leaving Ana in a dire state of poverty.

In the beginning, we focused on the intrapsychic work and establishing safety. When working with traumatized individuals, it is imperative that the consulting room become a "safe holding environment" (Winnicott, 1990). Creating such a space enabled Ana to name her problems, restore control, and establish a sense of safety. At this stage, we started following a banking model of therapy, in which she "invested" me with authority.

From the start of our therapy sessions, Ana and I discussed the unique nature of our psychotherapeutic relationship. Our work together consisted of establishing trust, learning to love another, and ultimately leaving the relationship. Since the therapeutic relationship is a blueprint for all other relationships, it is imperative that the patient learns the necessary ingredients for healthy relationships: mutuality, collaboration, accountability, etc., and how to separate, how to safely leave a relationship they have outgrown.

We also focused on power and control issues as they pertained to her relationship. We talked about domestic violence and her associations regarding power. We analyzed what it means to be a victim. We also began talking about Ana's history. She revealed that she grew up in a poor family in Guinea-Bissau; her parents were not always present and available for her or her brothers. As a child, she was instructed not to question authority and told that it was her responsibility to help her parents in any way she could. Her duties were to care for her brothers, and as she got older, this meant to cook, wash, and clean for them. She recounted how her family was so poor that she and her siblings all slept in the same bed, "and since there were five of us, we had to sleep across with our feet sticking out."

We analyzed the meaning of her parents' inability to parent. We looked at her father's lack of commitment and her mother's anger toward him and herself, as well as her community's expectations regarding her mother. Whereas the father was allowed to have many families and had children out of wedlock without consequences, her mother was expected to work, maintain the house and accept his behavior. His unexpected heart attack when Ana was fifteen cut off her support, leaving her feeling abandoned.

Ana dealt with her childhood trauma of being inadequately cared for by her mother through denial and splitting. She blamed her mother for not caring for her but revered her father who died. As our relationship developed, powerful negative feelings arose for Ana. Initially, they were directed toward her mother, then toward herself, and finally toward me. She felt angry with her mother, whom she accused of not being able to properly care for her. Her anger toward her father was concealed through reaction formation, viewing him as a hero who died unexpectedly. She even created the fantasy that if he had lived, her life would have been immensely better. Ana also exhibited anger at herself for not confronting her mother and for not being able to "speak-up and stand-up" for herself throughout her life.

My scheduled vacation enabled us to talk about her increasing anger toward me as well. Ana was annoyed by my taking time off, which she saw as a symbol of uncaring, aggressive abandonment. Her demands, doubts, and anger at my absences revealed in the transference the qualities of the internalized primary object.[4] My transference interpretations of this material were at first rejected. Eventually, Ana was able to listen to and sit with this interpretation. After the anger, her transference with me became idealistic, and she began seeing me as her father, who left her behind. This offered us the opportunity to analyze her feelings regarding his death and also her idealization of him/me. She was then able to integrate negative stories about him into her narrative. No longer an idealized object, her father became a man who, although he allowed his daughter to pursue an education, was also an alcoholic who did not provide for his daughter and had two families.

Ana was sexually molested by a neighbor while growing up, but she never told anyone about the abuse because she was scared her family would blame her. This fear came from her own internalized "badness," an effect of the abuse. We analyzed her feelings regarding this act of aggression toward her body and how, in order to survive and create a sense of control, she created a narrative in which she blamed herself for the abuse. It took some time for her to admit her parents' inability to provide safety for her and how this paralleled her current relationship with her boyfriend. As with her parents, the relationship with her boyfriend was ambivalent. On the one hand, he provided some security —like her father, who did not stop her from obtaining an education—yet, the price for that security was physical and verbal abuse and neglect, as it was with her father.

We also analyzed how therapy offered something she did not have as a child: love, protection, and a place where she could "sort out" her thoughts.

Stage Two

As the therapy progresses, the therapist engages the patient in a dialogical process by which the patient begins to vocalize and give shape to an interpretation of the world that identifies their oppression. The therapist begins to slowly renounce their power while moving into a more collaborative stance. Through this process, the patient begins an analysis of their relationship to power and realizes certain patterns and dynamics. Since oppression leads to an increased sense of fatalism and powerlessness, this process of regaining power is essential to the process of liberation (Fanon, 2008; Memmi, 2013).

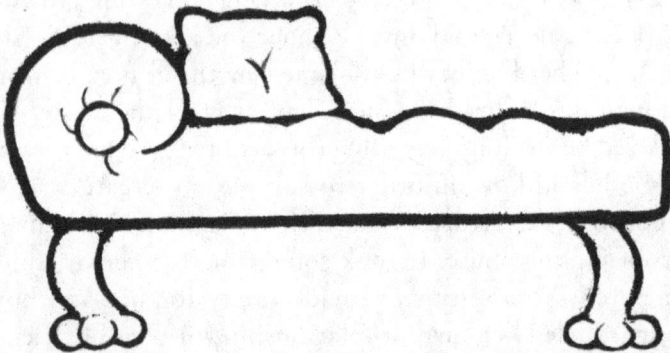

The therapist and the patient then co-interrogate the outlines of the world view that the patient voices while connecting it to the intrapsychic work. Language, the use of language, and an analysis of words and terms also enter the therapeutic hour. Therapist and patient analyze language and its "role in how power is gained and maintained" (Rivera et al., 2013, p. 34). The goal of therapy is not just analysis or adaptation of the individual to an oppressive system. The goal is liberation through active dialogue in which there is gradual decoding and de-ideologizing of the world. Martín-Baró saw the process of de-ideologizing the world as "helping people both retrieve their original experiences and return to their consciousness as objective and valuable data for decision-making" (Rivera et al., 2013, p. 35). The patient questions and analyzes how their perception of reality, while rooted in their lived experiences, is distorted by narratives and values dictated by a society that is invested in maintaining the status quo and imbalanced power relations. In this process, both patient and therapist also examine and reckon with their own role in maintaining oppressive conditions (Watkins & Shulman, 2008).

This process is rooted in Paulo Freire's (2000) concept of *conscientization*, meaning developing the capacity to critically reflect on the world in which we live, to consider and be mindful of psychological and sociopolitical realities. This practice is not something that the patient does alone but is rather a process that both patient and therapist engage in together. It's a praxis of transforming reality; therapy is the process through which one decodes the world. Patients begin to develop the ability to critically reflect, act, and reflect again to implement personal and political change. Reflexivity[5] is necessary with the therapist as well in order to remain committed to the practice of liberation (Ryan & Walsh, 2018).

The critical therapist is a radical therapist, in a Freireian sense, meaning they have made a "radical commitment to human liberation... [and] are not afraid to confront, to listen, to see the world unveiled. This person is not afraid to meet the people or to enter into dialogue with them" (2000, p. 39).

As the patient begins to develop critical consciousness, through an organic process of taking unarticulated aspects of their experience and posing them as problems to be questioned, the intrapsychic work is now revisited by posing questions to facilitate the interaction between the personal and the political.

As Ana continued looking at her life, she was able to understand her experiences in terms of traumatic identity, intergenerational abuse, and her introjections of bad objects. However, we went further than the intrapsychic work and started long conversations about race, class, gender, and colonialism. As our worked deepened, we started to incorporate critical-thinking skills through problem-solving approaches. We explored her world not only through her family dynamics and her fantasies and projections about them but also through a sociopolitical perspective. We looked at how ideology informed her view of the world and her role in that world. For example, this ideology told her that her poverty was her family's fault due to poor planning, and therefore they deserved to be impoverished. It also told her that the Catholic Church was a protective institution that would never hurt her, and therefore, when it sanctioned her abuse, it was right and it was she who was wrong.

We talked about Africa, specifically Guinea-Bissau, and the colonialism that contributed to Ana's family history. One way that I attempted to begin the process of co-interrogating this history was through her comment, spoken with an easiness in her voice, that "White people don't lie." I first asked how she came to this belief and why she is so convinced that White people are always honest. I challenged her regarding her belief in meritocracy by sharing my experience of privilege in the United States as a White woman. For example, at the time, I had never interviewed for a job where the interviewer was not White.

We also looked at how I, a White woman, was counseling her, a Black woman. She saw me as a rich accomplished woman who probably grew up on Fifth Avenue. After analyzing the fantasy that reinforced her ideology that all White people are wealthy and live in wealthy neighborhoods, I felt it was important—unlike a traditional therapist—to clarify my position regarding my privileges and status. I, too, was an immigrant like Ana. Yet, unlike Ana, I was privileged. My White Eastern European background opened doors that we both knew were closed to Ana. This offered us an opportunity to look at privilege and the way it operates in the United States.

At times, I felt uncomfortable. As a White woman, I wanted to work with Ana on these things, but I found myself trying to disavow my privileged position. I told myself that I, too, was an immigrant. I was helping her. I was not an accomplice to White supremacy. With time, I embraced my fears and realized that, like Ana, I, too, was shaped by my experiences. Instead of reserving my insights for supervision, I shared them with Ana. Together, we analyzed our place within White Patriarchy. We also continued our analytic work.

Ana's transference toward me shifted from the distant White therapist who had solutions to a "good enough mother" who offered her a safe space to "grow" and discover herself (Winnicott, 1990). With time, the quality of our transference relationship began to change. Ana's wishes for fusion increasingly changed to a transference dependence. We also worked more intensively on the correlation between the relationships of submission and the bad treatment she received from her boyfriend. She saw how passive submission had helped her survive her experience of sexual abuse. And she also felt guilty for that submission, for not being able to fight back. Ana understood how, as a child, she could not fight her abuser, yet she had difficulty forgiving herself for "letting it happen" and forgiving her body for betraying her.

Ana's self-punishment and blaming of her mother for her "lack of care" and of her father for "abandoning" her, occupied the entire affective field, leaving Ana no place for other feelings, such as hate, rage, and resentment toward her abusers (past and present). Her self-punishment allowed her to tolerate her current abuse since, on some level, she felt she deserved it because of her inherent badness. With time, however, Ana was able to verbalize these affects and move toward psychic integration.

Stage Three

In the last stage of therapy, the patient practices sharing power and overcoming authoritative and authoritarian tendencies, both within the initial therapeutic setup as well as within the patient's internal and external worlds. This part of the therapeutic dialogue is built upon humility, faith in each other's humanity, and love. In this last stage of therapy, the therapeutic relationship becomes one of cooperation, where two subjects meet to name the world (Freire, 2000, p. 167), and while the therapist maintains the stance of knowledge about psychology, the patient is empowered as the expert in their own life.

Liberation and empowerment meet in the therapeutic setting. The patient comes to understand their oppression as a function of structural inequalities and sees themselves as an agent of change. The patient becomes aware of their own power. As a result, the possibilities for action are expanded and become an open field for the expression of the patient's continued process of self-healing.

Critical therapy aims at individual and social transformation. The understanding by a patient that their oppression is partially constructed by social inequality is the first step. It is the role of the therapist to facilitate the continued interrogation of the notion of social inequality, revealing how the personal is political and how the patient's liberation and empowerment are related to and depend upon that of others. As a result of this process, the patient becomes an agent not only of personal change but of social transformation as well. Through their practice of liberation and empowerment, the patient can begin to create safe spaces for others while helping others to explore healthy personal and social identities. Critical therapy makes possible different kinds of relations to others, and those relations invite others to explore their own liberation and empowerment.

As Ana linked her experiences to social and historical realities, learning to connect the dots on her own, she came to understand how her ideas of herself and her relationships were shaped by long histories of racism, capitalism, and colonialism. She started to question her society's construction of gender roles and the inferiority of women. She realized that much of what she believed to be natural or ordained by God was in fact not natural at all—that women were not naturally inferior and that Whites were not naturally better than Blacks. We talked about ways in which capitalism, in order to excuse the gross injustices created by a free-market economy, constructed a narrative in which poor people are lazy and the rich are hard-working. These insights alleviated some of her negative views about herself as a Black woman. She began seeing how her narrative of poverty and her reliance on an abusive boyfriend were tied in with stories about women's roles, White privilege, and class issues.

Ana began researching more and more about colonialism. One day in session she burst out with anger: "You know, I began wondering where did the Catholic Church come up with all that rice? How come they had all that land? How come they were all White? And then it hit me... they stole it from us." She came to see her parents as people, forgiving them for their shortcomings and understanding the interplay between their lack of parenting skills, their poverty, and colonial control. She did not blame the White Man for all her grievances, but she clearly understood his control and involvement in them.

Through the process of investigating her own oppression, Ana became an ardent advocate. She thought about other women in her country. She started to talk about the importance of women's education as it relates to independence and empowerment. She also saw connections between poverty, religion, and reproductive rights. She better understood her mother's position and wanted to repair her relationship with her and understand her struggles as a mother and a woman. She began to see how her mother's position within society might have affected her ability to parent.

When it came to her boyfriend, her reluctance to report him to the authorities continued to be a point of resistance for us. Analytically, we talked about what he represented for her. He was a male figure who, although he had treated her badly, had not abandoned her. Unlike everyone she knew, he was willing to "stick it out with me." Much like her father, he offered both support and huge disappointment. We talked about her fears regarding abandonment, how his verbal abuse reinforced negative feelings about herself and her ability to be loved. As Ana was able to integrate the good/bad father, she was also able to see her boyfriend in a different light. She understood that although he provided some support, he was also an abuser who hurt her. We worked through the meaning of her fantasies of "what if" she had a different family environment or a caring boyfriend. The saddest part was Ana's realization of the lack of financial options if she left her boyfriend. She knew that once she broke up with him, all financial support would end. Ana could have qualified for immigrant status under the Violence Against Women Act if she had been willing to cooperate with the authorities about the abuse. However, because Ana was unwilling to report the abuse, she could not obtain a permanent visa in the United States that might have offered her the ability to work and provide for herself. Since she lacked funds and wanted to finish her schooling, going home was not an option either.

We analyzed Ana's justified reluctance to report her boyfriend to the authorities. We both knew her decision was based on mistrust and fear of abuse when it comes to authorities in general and the police in particular, especially in communities of color. Many women of color simply will not call the police for fear of what will happen to themselves or their abusive partner in the hands of law enforcement officers. Unfortunately, the strategies we've designed to combat sexual violence within communities, are not mindful of or linked to strategies that combat violence directed against communities —in such forms as police brutality, prisons, racism, homophobia, and economic exploitation.

With time, Ana began separating from her boyfriend, a shift fostered by Ana's introjection of the good objects and her realization that I would not abandon her. She was now able to integrate all of her history and to see her boyfriend as a troubled individual and her parents as deeply flawed and human. Some financial support from a local social service agency helped to facilitate her departure. The financial support opened Ana's eyes regarding the lack of financial options available to poor women and women of color to seek to escape abusive relationships. Ana also recognized her own privileged position within her culture. As an educated woman, possibilities for employment were much better for her than for someone without a college degree.

Learning to say goodbye to each other, to leave therapy, was an essential component of my work with Ana. In critical therapy, the process of termination happens naturally, where both patient and therapist start noticing the shift in weekly sessions. Having worked through issues and learned the necessary tools to critically analyze and understand their patterns, combined with an experiential shift and transformation, patients no longer come to sessions in crisis or to work something through. At this last stage of therapy, sessions look more like the time friends spend conversing and sharing stories.

As the therapy was organically coming to an end, I discussed with Ana the possibility of presenting her case and our work together to the world. She was excited by this, and together we collaborated on telling the story of our journey. After reading my first draft of the case presentation, she added some points. We also discussed the obvious shift in our dynamic since she now saw me more as a collaborator than an authority figure.

Today, Ana has finished her degree and has obtained a work visa. She is hoping to make enough money so that she can return to Guinea-Bissau, and she hopes to become an advocate for women's rights. She wants to share her experience of the United States and her insight regarding colonialism, sexism, and oppression with others in the hope that she can ignite change in her country. She also wants to tell them that America is not a country paved with gold and that racism and sexism are alive and well here. She now knows that White people lie, that we robbed her country and exploited her people and, in many ways, continue to do so. She also knows that some White people recognize this and are willing to stand in solidarity with her. She has a better understanding of her family dynamics. She knows violence is wrong, women can be leaders, and that negative self-esteem may lead to abusive relationships. More importantly, she understands how psychic connections, unconscious dreams, and sociopolitical realities are interrelated.

Liberation and Empowerment
Meet in the Clinical Setting

Much like critical pedagogy and liberation psychology, critical therapy enables the therapist and the patient to begin to learn about their oppression through reflection. Critical therapy becomes the place where patients learn how to become critical agents who question and negotiate relationships between theory and practice. The therapist sees this as an expansion of democracy and helps patients understand how the current capitalist, settler colonialist system influences and constructs certain structural rules.

As patient and therapist explore personal and structural changes, patients may begin to reformulate the narratives of their lives and see possibilities for change; they may in fact see themselves as agents of change. Therapy is transformed into a sphere where patients find support to both question and assert their own power in personal relationships—with their partners, friends, children, and others more or *less* powerful than them. Therapy also becomes the place where survivors of trauma begin to understand their own power as critically engaged citizens and agents of change.

In critical therapy, the consulting room becomes the place where patient and therapist begin to look at the nexus between social conditions and psychological problems, where they can focus on internal problems as well as social transformations. To be clear, our work is not about forcing our patients to be political activists but about asking them questions regarding their personal feelings as well as the society and world we live in; it is about making them aware of the social conflicts they struggle with every day and how their story fits into the larger picture. Perhaps, the biggest lesson they will learn is that they are not alone. In this manner, practice becomes revolutionary.

In doing so, patients move from a victim outlook to a survivor framework and begin to see their own transformative power. Aside from offering therapeutic comfort and therapeutic insights, therapy also becomes a performative practice where patients actively reflect on their own power and their relationship to the ongoing project of an unfinished democracy. Seeing themselves as active participants, fully capable of self-governing, patients strive to further expand democratic societies to include (for example): free, fair, and frequent elections; effective participation; and inclusive citizenship (Dahl, 2005; 2006). Having learned in therapy how to trust their experiences and co-exist with another, patients are now able to engage, participate, and collectively self-govern. It is precisely this relationship between democracy and therapy that is hopeful for survivors everywhere.

Chapter Three

Love and Psychotherapy

A RANDOM sampling of articles on the topic of love and psycho-therapy reveals that most scholarly works, like most therapists, adopt an impersonal and clinical approach to the question of love in therapy. Although these articles discuss the multiple complexities of being in therapy, including erotic love and countertransference, the question of how we, as clinicians, approach love in sessions with our patients is avoided or dealt with indirectly if it is recognized at all.

Love is an essential human emotion present in countless daily interactions of care, solicitude, empathy, and solidarity. Yet, our society seldom talks about love without connecting it to sex or romance. Contemporary society recasts relation-ships of love and responsibility, such as those of parents to children, as relations of authority, and it recasts relationships of empathy and solidarity as charity for those less fortunate. The dominant capitalist ethic has shifted the focus of society from care for another whom we love and want to share with to an erotic or romantic fantasy of being consumed or possessed —a fantasy that is easier to market and turn into profit.

For our patients and for us, love is often a complicated topic. It is no surprise, given our society's long histories of trauma and abuse, coupled with the fact that we seldom talk about cooperation, mutuality, and non-romantic love, that the topic of loving is difficult. From magazine covers to movies and novels, we are bombarded with romantic notions of love. Self-help books teach us either how to love ourselves or how to find "the one" and experience a relationship filled with romance. What is lost in the conversation is love without romance, love without sex, love for another rooted in friendship, mutuality, and cooperation. Yet, it is there, always already present in our daily interactions, often unrecognized. Borrowing a phrase from Colin Ward (1973), it's "like a seed beneath the snow, buried under the weight of the state and its bureaucracy, capitalism and its waste...."

Reading through the countless articles on the subject of transference and erotic love as they enter the therapeutic hour does not offer much guidance, serving only to highlight the complexity of the study of non-erotic love. As Bodenheimer (2011, p. 39) points out:

> There are many reasons not to discuss or study the reality of non-erotic love in the psychotherapeutic relationship. These include conceptual struggles regarding the actual meaning of "non-erotic love"; linguistic difficulties that are byproducts of the evocative tenor of the word "love" itself; and the obstacles produced by researching a concept that is so largely defined by its subjective nature. But perhaps the most powerful reason to avoid the complicated presence of love in the therapeutic relationship is the very reason it must be deeply understood and scrutinized: It is an ethical minefield.

Perhaps this minefield exists because, from the therapist's perspective, to talk about love in psychotherapy is to talk about oneself and one's professional boundaries, which requires honesty and a lot of self-awareness and reflection.

Freud (1993), although recognizing the importance and centrality of love in our lives, saw love as a distraction and wanted to practice therapy free from what he saw as a counter-transferential emotion. When urged by Ferenczi (De Forest, 1954) to question his beliefs regarding the role of love in treatment, Freud quickly rejected the suggestion (Cabre, 1998). Perhaps Freud's reluctance might be explained as fear, since at the time, he was writing his 1905 paper *Fragment of an Analysis of a Case of Hysteria*, in which he explored the case of Ida Bauer, or "Dora." This case was difficult for Freud, especially since his own countertransferential feelings were not fully processed or analyzed (Csibi, 2019; O'Donnell, 2006).

Ferenczi, however, did speak about love in psychotherapy. In 1920 at The Hague, he stated that "the progress of the cure bears no relation to the depth of the patient's theoretical insight, nor to the memories laid bare" (Stanton 1991, p. 133). Instead, his method was "developed to the fullest when he recognized that genuine sincerity and empathic attunement were the essential ingredients to reach a traumatized individual" (Rachman, 1998, p. 265).

Ferenczi believed that unless the therapist is willing to bridge the distance between themselves and the patient, cure is impossible. Whereas Freud saw distance as part of the therapeutic technique, Ferenczi saw it as a defense. He argued that patients are often deprived of love and care, and indeed it is through an experience of love and care that healing is possible. He believed that treatment outcomes were directly related to the amount of love given by the therapist to the patient.

Since then, research on this mutuality has flourished, especially within the interpersonal field of psychoanalysis.

Shaw's (2003) historical analysis of the understanding of analytic love brought him to the belief that "analytic love is indeed complicated and dangerous, and like all loving, carries the potential for devastating disappointment..." but, he goes on to say: "at the heart of this endeavor, I believe, for both analyst and analysand, is a search for love, for the sense of being lovable, for the remobilization of thwarted capacities to give love and to receive love" (2003, pp. 252, 275).

In critical therapy, love develops over time. At first, the therapeutic relationship is unequal, as the patient invests feelings and shares emotions with the therapist, who maintains emotional distance in order for the transference to develop. Among other things, transference offers the therapist an opportunity to understand how the patient has experienced and sees love. Together, they critically look at patterns, narratives, and the ways that past unresolved experiences may negatively influence current behavior, so that the patient can lead a more authentic life.

Trust is essential in the therapeutic relationship. It develops as the patient experiences the therapist as someone who is able to be vulnerable, express emotions, and be comfortable with love. Over time, the patient feels and understands that the therapist is taking a therapeutic journey of transformation with them and is not just there as a neutral expert.

As the therapy develops and the relationship deepens, there is a switch toward more collaboration, the sharing of power, and overcoming the authoritative and authoritarian tendencies in the initial therapeutic setup, in the patient and therapist, and in the world at large.

The experience of love and mutuality emerges. And in the last stage of critical therapy, much in line with Ferenczi, love becomes more apparent, as it is one of the ingredients of therapy. Having developed a relationship in which patient and therapist share stories while interrogating the world together, love becomes a part of a real connection. And through this process, both patient and therapist are changed.

Love for the patient and with the patient is the ultimate gift of therapy. Both patient and therapist change as a result of this intimate relationship, developed over time amid stories of horror, anger, shame, fear, as well as beauty, hope and healing. Learning how to be with an Other in the therapeutic hour is the blueprint of the art of loving; the art of being with someone, of accepting the perfect imperfections of an Other, of being together.

Chapter Four

The Sliding Scale: Practicing a Politics of Equity

THE SUBJECT of money, whether we like it or not, is a part of psychotherapy. Conversations around money start early in the process, as patients and therapists discuss and agree on fees prior to coming for a consultation. Here at the outset, key but not at all simple questions arise, such as: How do we, as clinicians, decide what we should charge for a psychotherapy session? How do patients decide how much each session is "worth" financially? How should the reality of staggering and unprecedented income inequality in our country factor into our decisions to these questions?

In the United States, disparities in wealth are justified by a neoliberal ideology[6] claiming that success, as measured by financial prosperity, is a result of one's hard work and dedication. Differences in class, race, gender, and ability, among others, are explained away or even suppressed in ways that support the belief that poverty is a personal individual failure rather than a social artifact and systemic problem (Salecl, 2008; 2019). As a result, discussing how much money one has, whether inherited or earned, is not an easy topic, as it is ultimately tied to core beliefs underlying one's self-esteem and personal sense of worth. I have witnessed how uncomfortable a patient becomes when discussing finances, for example, naming the amount of money they received as a result of a salary increase or bonus. Yet this same patient may have little reservation sharing their most intense emotional fears or sexual desires. We've all experienced this taboo around the subject of money. It is considered improper or poor etiquette to ask about someone's financial situation. For example, how many of us actually know how much money our dear friends have or the salaries of our coworkers? And, as you continue to read this chapter, I invite you to notice if any of these unexpected feelings arise in you.

Money is a stand-in for many other things: worth, competence, freedom, prestige, power, masculinity, and control (Turkel, 1988; Schwartz, 2016). This leaves most of us, including psychotherapists, feeling embarrassed or conflicted about discussing it (Krueger, 1986, p. vii). It's no wonder the subject of money is "perhaps the most ignored subject in the practice, literature, and training of psychotherapy" (Trachtman, 1999, p. 276). In social work and psychology graduate programs or clinical training institutes, there is little talk about financial matters.

Just as they create the therapeutic frame by setting the time, establishing boundaries, and explaining free association, etc., therapists are encouraged in their clinical training to be open with their patients about fees (Newman, 2005). Transparency around money opens the door to other difficult or socially taboo conversations. Yet, for many therapists, the topic of money—how much to charge per session—raises internal conflicts around self-worth, the desire to help others, and the realities of earning a sustainable living wage. There is a perceived tension or anxiety felt between being seen as a helper or healer and being able to earn a living and live a comfortable life. Psychoanalytically, we've been told that fee-setting is revelatory of the therapist's relationship to greed, neediness, dependency, and power (Willock et al., 2009). Setting and explaining the fee structure to patients reveals something about the therapist's values. It also documents in a very tangible and experiential way, the therapist's politics and commitment to social justice.

Just as charging too much money for psychotherapy can be seen as greedy on the part of the therapist, there is also a belief that psychotherapy will not be effective if it is free. There is a myth, especially in the history of psychoanalysis, that Freud believed fees should be set high enough to motivate the patient to do the difficult work of analysis. However, as Danto (2005) documents, Freud and other analysts at the time who had a commitment to social justice believed in treating the poor for free. In fact, even during Freud's time, there were outpatient centers providing free mental health services to those who could not afford them.

Contrary to the myth that higher payment means more investment on the part of the patient (or the therapist for that matter), research shows that patients who pay a higher fee do not benefit more from therapy than those who do not (Clark & Sims, 2014). In fact, when "diagnosis and socio-economic status were controlled, there was no significant difference in therapeutic outcome on the basis of fee" (Bishop & Eppolito, 1992; Lasky, 1984, p. 290). As psychotherapists know well, how much we get paid per hour is not a reflection of the quality of our care; patients pay for our time, not for our emotional investment in them.

When it comes to establishing a set fee, most psychotherapists in private practice charge based on the average rate in their geographical area; others charge only high fees, and some charge a standard fee but offer a sliding scale for those who cannot afford the set price (Tudor, 1998). It should be noted that the sliding-scale model offered by most psychotherapists slides only downward and never upward. Historically, this model of paying based on a sliding scale originated in Europe in an effort to avoid commercializing healthcare and medicine and ensure that surgeons charged "reasonable" fees. European law restricted a doctor's ability to bill for their services, and most doctors charged patients according to what they could pay. However, this practice was not and is not a part of American law (Hall & Schneider, 2008).

In the United States, the growth of private insurance companies brought standardized fees for physicians, prevented surcharges, and also enabled some discounts (Hall & Schneider, 2008). It is not widely known by people outside the medical profession that insurance companies often negotiate rates with doctors and hospitals, while uninsured patients, who do not have the same leverage or ability to negotiate end up paying more. The current sliding-scale model ends up charging the most amount of money to patients who can least afford it: Primary care physicians charge uninsured patients one-third to a half more than they receive from insurance (Hall & Schneider, 2008). Instead of charging the most to those who can least afford it or simply refusing to treat people who do not meet a particular ability-to-pay threshold, what if everyone paid their fair share? What if the sliding scale moved not only downward but also upward?

As a practicing psychotherapist, I know the need for and importance of high-quality psychotherapy and how it can save one's life. Yet, a lack of financial resources makes such therapy inaccessible for too many. COVID-19 has shown how income inequality affects our daily lives. As loneliness and isolation continue to grow exponentially in our society, we also see a need for mental health services, especially talk therapy. If we want to end the gross inequalities of capitalism, the revolution must also begin on the couch.

For those embracing a commitment to a more equitable world, providing psychotherapy services requires that every patient pay according to their income and resources, with no minimum or maximum per session. In other words, one session may cost $50, $500, or $5000 for example. Using this method, patients with greater income and resources help to make therapy accessible for those with less financial resources while ensuring a comfortable living for the psychotherapist. Further, this scale enables patients and therapists to deal with income inequality in a very tangible way, enacting a politics of equity that ensures that necessary, sometimes life-saving, healthcare services will not be mediated by the market.

Many may assume that this proposition is unattainable, that affluent patients will turn away. However, together with like-minded psychotherapists, we've been using this sliding-scale model for over a decade at the Critical Therapy Institute in New York City, treating patients across the socioeconomic spectrum. Our practice accounts for expenses, family composition, and other factors, so that every patient pays the same percentage of relative income and resources for their psychotherapy hour. By resources, we mean intergenerational wealth and other holdings, since accounting only for a patient's earnings while ignoring their full financial situation would not be equitable. In addition, to remain sustainable and inclusive, every therapist in our practice reserves a certain number of slots for low, medium, and high-paying patients. To consider only income while ignoring wealth leads to inadvertently sacrificing a low-fee slot for a patient who really needs it.

Although the sliding-scale model is a fairer and more equitable model than most fee-setting standards patients are accustomed to, I have seen how uncomfortable patients become when it is introduced to them in practice. Even for progressive-minded people who intellectually understand and support an income redistribution model in theory, there is often a visceral reaction, an "it's not fair that rich people pay more" response. However, the scale is designed in such a way that everyone pays the same percentage of their income and financial resources for the 50-minute psychotherapy session.

The sliding-scale model also ensures that psychotherapists earn livable, comfortable wages while doing important, sometimes life-saving work. The notion of a livable, comfortable wage is key, as most therapists working with people who are experiencing poverty work long hours for very little pay. Burnout is common, and some end up leaving the profession altogether. The false dichotomy between doing the good work of treating only marginalized and disenfranchised people in overworked and underpaying mental health clinics versus "selling-out" in private practice and working with only high-paying patients helps to perpetuate rather than challenge our current system. When therapists insist that these are the only two viable options, we fail to think beyond the false binaries of capitalism and unconsciously position the rich against the poor. Instead, a sliding-scale model rooted in solidarity and mutual aid ensures that we all do better.

When we practice a politics of equity in psychotherapy, we are able to work with and help patients from all walks of life. In our waiting rooms, the division between the privileged and the less privileged is softened, as people from different racial, ethnic, and socioeconomic backgrounds encounter each other. For more affluent patients, this might be a rare opportunity to be sitting across from someone who is affected by poverty. In those moments, the invisible Other becomes visible. As one low-income patient of color told me:

"When I come up the elevator and ring this doorbell to this fancy office, I see how White people look at me. They wonder if I belong, and I confidently smile a silent 'yes' as I ring your office." For less affluent patients, this is a moment of affirmation of their dignity.

Conversations about the sliding scale offer everyone who seeks therapy with a critical therapist a chance for deep critical inquiry into their own relationship to money. Family history is visited; political history and economic values are critically examined. For affluent patients, this is a rare opportunity to discuss and revisit their relationship and personal history with regard to wealth and to expose, analyze and question how they embody their politics. It is rare because when it comes to psychotherapy and money, only the less affluent, the oppressed, and the marginalized are forced to have these conversations—out of necessity. When the sliding scale only goes downward in order to help those less economically privileged, the burden of difficult conversations around money exists only for those patients. The more affluent simply pay the set fee—and miss an opportunity to deeply interrogate their own feelings around wealth, worth, and power.

Therapeutically, conversations around self-worth and income are a necessary part of any good psychotherapy, even if the patient seems reluctant to bring them up at first. As psychotherapists know, it is never just about the money but about the feelings that money can hide. In practice, both affluent and less affluent patients struggle with their financial situations, consummated by feelings of shame and guilt or grandiosity. Conversations around wealth and power are a necessary part of the therapeutic dialogue, and to ignore them is to miss an opportunity for critically investigating one's ideology, values, and place within our current political and social structures. By opening the conversation early on, we acknowledge how fundamentally economic factors deeply affect and impact psychological well-being.

Many affluent patients carry a deep shame around wealth, feel undeserving of it, and often hide their financial means while struggling with self-worth. In our society, which reveres wealth and what it can buy and has bought into the myth that what we earn reflects how hard we work or how smart we are, the silence around inherited wealth is problematic. As one of my patients, who stands to inherit three million dollars from her mother, told me: "I cannot accept that money unless I make more money on my own. I have to prove my worth." After many months of being deeply and psychologically unhappy at work, she revealed that an unpaid leave of absence (even at the cost of her well-being) was not an option for her, as she would see herself as a "failure" if she relied on her mother's money. To admit financial need, she painfully explained to me, would be an affirmation of her inability to do it on her own, to pull herself up by her own bootstraps.

For therapists, the sliding scale brings up feelings around their own self-worth, as well as the value of their services. Many therapists who have practiced for many years with a set fee or in low-income social service agencies experience trepidation and visceral self-doubt once they encounter a high-paying patient, asking themselves, "Am I worth it? Is this session good enough?" Such feelings reveal how much neoliberal ideology and the value of money are embedded deep within our minds. We believe we are good enough therapists when working with people experiencing poverty, yet as soon as we are treating patients with deep financial privileges, insecurity and doubt creep in. All of a sudden, clinicians feel that they need to perform more, that every session should be spectacular, insightful, and generative, even though we know that the hard work of psychotherapy involves learning how to sit with things and be in relationship with another in the midst of many challenges and feelings.

Analyzing both the therapist's and patient's relationship to money requires vulnerability, transparency, honesty, and a deep analysis of how we may feel around money. More importantly, this analysis highlights sometimes deeply buried conflicts around what we feel versus what we think. Critically analyzing our values is a necessary part of any psychotherapy, as the political affects the personal. Healing, mental health and wellness cannot be achieved independent of political realities. Personal and political transformations are always intertwined.

Notes

1. I am intentionally using the word *patient* to describe the uniqueness and responsibility found in a therapeutic relationship. Psychotherapists do not simply provide a service; we are active participants in the process of healing. There is a significant power differential in this relationship that is unique. Our patients share intimate things about themselves and the level of trust and responsibility on the part of the therapist is not adequately captured by the term *client*.

2. For the sake of confidentiality, names and other biographical details have been changed.

3. The term *banking model* was coined by Freire (2000) to describe traditional education, where the teacher "deposits" information into students.

4. An internalized primary object is a mental image of a person (usually the mother or primary caretaker) that is now experienced as inside the self.

5. Reflexivity is an educational approach used in critical pedagogy. It involves a critical assessment of how subjectivity, environment, power, and context construct knowledge. Without reflexivity, psychotherapy becomes a process where the therapist merely transfers values and practices that are part of dominant culture and in service of the status quo.

6. Neoliberal ideology is defined by David Harvey as "a theory of political economic practices that proposes that human well-being can best be advanced by liberating individual entrepreneurial freedoms and skills within an institutional framework characterized by strong private property rights, free markets, and free trade" (2005, p. 2).

References

Chapter 1. What is Critical Therapy, and How Is It Different from Other Therapies?

Giddens, A. (1984). *The constitution of society: Outline of the theory of structuration*. University of California Press.

Chapter 2. Ana: A Case History

Burton, C., & Kagan, C. (2005). Liberation social psychology: Learning from Latin America. *Journal of Community & Applied Social Psychology, 15*, 63–78.

Dahl, R. (2005). What political institutions does large-scale democracy require? *Political Science Quarterly, 120*(2), 187–198.

Dahl, R. (2006). *On political equality*. Yale University Press.

Fabri, M. R. (2001). Reconstructing safety: Adjustments to the therapeutic frame in the treatment of survivors of political torture. *Professional Psychology: Research and Practice, 32*(5), 452.

Fabri, M., Joyce, M., Black, M., & González, M. (2009). Caring for torture survivors: The Marjorie Kovler Center. In C. E. Stout (Ed.) *The new humanitarians: Inspiration, innovations, and blueprints for visionaries, Vol. 1, Changing Global Health Inequities* (pp. 157–187). Praeger Publishers/Greenwood Publishing Group.

Fanon, F. (2008). *Black skin, White masks*. Grove Press.

Freire, P. (2000). *Pedagogy of the oppressed*. M. Bergman Ramos (Trans.). Continuum.

Gates, A. (1988). Letter from Alice Gates.
www.oberlin.edu/external/EOG/SEPA/Gatesletter.html

Lynd, S. (2012). *Accompanying: Pathways to social change*. PM Press.

Memmi, A. (2013). *The colonizer and the colonized*. Routledge.

Rivera, E. T., Maldonado, J., & Alarcon, L. (2013). From Vygotsky to Martín Baró: Dealing with language and liberation during the supervision process. *Universal Journal of Psychology*. *1*(2): 32–40.

Ryan, A., & Walsh, T. (2018). *Reflexivity and critical pedagogy* (pp. 1–14). Brill Sense.

Watkins, M., & Shulman, H. (2008). Symptoms and psychologies in cultural context. In Toward psychologies of liberation (pp. 53–63). Palgrave Macmillan, London.

Winnicott, D. W. (1990). *Family and individual development*. Routledge.

Chapter 3. Love and Psychotherapy

Bodenheimer, D. (2011). An examination of the historical and current perceptions of love in the psychotherapeutic dyad. *Clinical Social Work Journal*, 39(1), 39–49.

Cabre, L. (1998). Ferenczi's contribution to the concept of countertransference. *International Forum of Psychoanalysis*, 7, 247–255.

Csibi, E. (2019). What did we learn from the dora case? Transference and countertransference in the dyadic relationship.

De Forest, I. (1954). The leaven of love: A development of the psychoanalytic theory and technique of Sándor Ferenczi.

Freud, S. (1993). Observations on transference-love: Further recommendations on the technique of psycho-analysis III. *The Journal of psychotherapy practice and research*, 2(2), 171.

O'Donnell, B. (2006). Discovering transference.

Rachman, A. W. (1998, December). Judicious self-disclosure by the psychoanalyst. *International Forum of Psychoanalysis*, 7(4), 263–270.

Shaw, D. (2003). On the therapeutic action of analytic love. *Contemporary Psychoanalysis*, 39(2), 251–278.

Stanton, M. (1991). *Sándor Ferenczi: Reconsidering active intervention*. Jason Aronson.

Ward, C. (1973). *Anarchy in action*. Harper and Row.

Chapter 4. The Sliding Scale:
Practicing a Politics of Equity

Bishop, D. R., & Eppolito, J. M. (1992). The clinical management of client dynamics and fees for psychotherapy: Implications for research and practice. *Psychotherapy: Theory, Research, Practice, Training*, 29(4), 545.

Clark, P., & Sims, P. L. (2014). The practice of fee setting and collection: Implications for clinical training programs. *The American Journal of Family Therapy*, 42(5), 386–397.

Danto, E. A. (2005). *Freud's free clinics: Psychoanalysis & social justice, 1918–1938*. New York: Columbia University Press.

Hall, M. A., & Schneider, C. E. (2008). Learning from the legal history of billing for medical fees. *Journal of General Internal Medicine*, 23(8), 1257.

Harvey, D. (2005). *A brief history of neoliberalism*. Oxford.

Krueger, D. W. (Ed.). (1986). *The last taboo: Money as symbol and reality in psychotherapy and psychoanalysis*. Routledge.

Lasky, E. (1984). Psychoanalysts' and psychotherapists' conflicts about setting fees. *Psychoanalytic Psychology*, 1(4), 289.

Newman, S. S. (2005). Considering fees in psychodynamic psychotherapy: Opportunities for residents. *Academic Psychiatry*, 29(1), 21–28.

Piketty, T., & Saez, E. (2001). *Income inequality in the United States, 1913–1998*. National Bureau of Economic Research. http://nber.org/papers/w8467

Salecl, R. (2008). The nature of the event in late capitalism. *Cardozo Law Review, 29*(5), 2333–2345.

Salecl, R. (2019). Choice and consumerism. In *Routledge handbook of psychoanalytic political theory* (pp. 307–315). Routledge.

Schwartz, S. L. (2016). How Money Talks by Lesley Murdin London: Karnac Books, 2012, 200 pp. *International Journal of Applied Psychoanalytic Studies, 13*(1), 85–88.

Trachtman, R. (1999). The money taboo: Its effects in everyday life and in the practice of psychotherapy. *Clinical Social Work Journal, 27*(3), 275–288.

Tudor, K. (1998). Value for money? Issues of fees in counselling and psychotherapy. *British Journal of Guidance and Counselling, 26*(4), 477–493.

Turkel, A. R. (1988). Money as a mirror of marriage. *Journal of the American Academy of Psychoanalysis, 16*(4), 525–535.

Willock, B., Curtis, R. C., & Bohm, L. C. (Eds.). (2009). *Taboo or not taboo: Forbidden thoughts, forbidden acts in psychoanalysis and psychotherapy*. Karnac Books.

Acknowledgements

EVERYONE WHO has been a part of my life has been a part of this book. No one writes a book alone. The myth of doing anything alone is just that: a myth. We are products of experiences, as we carry fragments of people we encounter throughout our lives, and the process of writing a book is no different. From ideas that were born out of countless conversations with others, from editing, to the delivery people who brought me groceries so that I can save time and focus on my writing, everyone has helped, and for that I thank you all!

To my patients for helping me create Critical Therapy as a theory. I thank you for the privilege of allowing me to be a part of your life in such a special and unique way, and for trusting me. Your strength, courage and desire to heal humbles me. To Ana for allowing me to tell parts of your story in the case presentation, for our collaboration together, and for choosing *me* to be the one to accompany *you* on your journey of healing and transformation.

To my fellow clinicians at the Critical Therapy Institute who believe in the transformative power of psychotherapy to change the world, who embody our values and who've trusted me enough to become an "us." Vileti 'Akolo, Rebecca Gruia, Sarah Knight, Yolaine Menyard, Monica Roldan, Jené Toussaint, Sherrie Waller, and Brenda Zubay. To Elizabeth Keeney for taking this manuscript on her vacation and returning with much needed suggestions. To Eleni Zimiles for reading and also finding another pair of eyes to help us edit parts of this book that were difficult. To Michael Madormo an awesome educator, a close reader and a much-needed ear when I needed to vent. Kate Barrow for your organizational skills, your much needed sincerity and ethics; you keep me grounded. Megan Chinn my coworker, friend and sister in struggle; together we went from two people talking about what critical therapy could be, to building an Institute. Your gentleness, your thoughtfulness, your ability to "slow me down" is greatly appreciated.

To V (fka Eve Ensler), Daniel José Gaztambide, George Zafiriadis, Janet Plotkin Bornstein, Armin Baier, Carolyn Jacoby, and Marie C. Wilson. To Ed Levy for editing the final manuscript with precision and care. To Mỹ Tâm Nguyễn for making me a better speaker and encouraging me to think big. To Gareth Southwell who helped so much and was continuously reassuring through this process.

To Nadira Ramcharan for taking care of our family and giving me the much-needed space to write.

To Sucheta Dasrat, Sadhana Duncan, Peter Thompson and Florence Mui for a lifetime of friendship.

To Mom—for teaching me how to wrestle with power.

To Dad—for always believing in me.

To Damian for teaching me how to believe in myself, for filling my life with joy and laughter, while also taking care of our home day in and day out; for editing this manuscript over and over again, and for always challenging me when I needed it the most, but could hear it the least. You truly accompany me on this journey called life.

To Adriana for reminding me to believe in others, to love more, to slow down, and to play. I will always be grateful for you.

Bios

Megan Chinn, MSW, LCSW, is a licensed psychotherapist with years of experience providing therapy in various community-based settings, including high schools, residential homeless facilities, and LGBTQ youth services organizations. She practices holistic psychotherapy with an emphasis on trauma-informed care, while drawing on mindfulness, intersectionality, and harm-reduction approaches. Megan's clinical focus is on the application of critical race theory, transformative justice, and spirituality within the therapeutic context. Currently, she is developing interventions bridging critical therapy theory with transformative justice practices.

Silvia M. Dutchevici, MA, LCSW, is president and founder of the Critical Therapy Institute. A trained psychotherapist, Dutchevici (pronounced "doot-KAY-vitch"), created critical therapy on perceiving a need for the theory and practice of psychology to reflect how race, class, gender, and religion intersect with psychological conflicts. She is a founding board member of Black Women's Blueprint and a member of the Physicians for Human Right's Asylum Network, where she conducts psychological evaluations documenting evidence of torture and persecution for survivors fleeing danger in their home countries. She trained at the Bellevue/NYU Survivors of Torture Program, the Parent Child Center of the New York Psychoanalytic Society, and the New York Freudian Society. Dutchevici has a master's degree in social work from New

York University and a master's degree in psychology from the New School, and a bachelor's degree in religious studies and political science from Fordham University. She has lectured and presented throughout the country on critical therapy, including at Fordham and NYU, and has been featured in the *Washington Post*, *The Wall Street Journal*, *Psychology Today*, *The Guardian*, *International Business Times*, and *Women's Health*.

Daniel José Gaztambide, PsyD, is the assistant director of clinical training in the Department of Clinical Psychology at the New School for Social Research, where he is also the director of the Frantz Fanon Center for Intersectional Psychology. Originally from Puerto Rico, he is a practitioner in private practice and a psychoanalytic candidate at the NYU-Postdoctoral Program in Psychotherapy and Psychoanalysis. He is the author of the book *A People's History of Psychoanalysis: From Freud to Liberation Psychology*, and was featured in the documentary *Psychoanalysis in el Barrio*.

George Zafiriadis (aka @squiddysprinkle), an openly gay NYC native artist, is an illustrator, comic and concept artist. Much of his work centers around creating a safe space for LGBTQ+ people, and advocating for mental health and sexual wellness.

Index